GEODE

poetry by

Ona Gritz

MAIN STREET RAG PUBLISHING COMPANY
CHARLOTTE, NORTH CAROLINA

Library of Congress Control Number: 2013952235

ISBN: 978-1-59948-449-5

Produced in the United States of America

Main Street Rag
PO Box 690100
Charlotte, NC 28227
www.MainStreetRag.com

ACKNOWLEDGMENTS

Many thanks to the editors of the following publications in which some of these poems have appeared:

The American Voice: "In Rockaway"
The Apple Valley Review: "After the Ultrasound," "Mr. Rogers"
Bellevue Literary Review: "Hemiplegia II" as "Hemiplegia"
Concise Delight: "Birth Room Mirror," "Just This Once"
Damselfly Press: "Slow Cooker Stew"
Flashquake: "Fever Spike," "Weekend Fair," "Beach 27th Street"
Inglis House Poetry Workshop: "First Anniversary," "Passing"
Lily: "Before Books" as "One Writer's Beginnings"
Literary Mama: "Boy Child," "Family Bed," "Testing the Seams,"
    "The Impatient Mother," "The Night We Decide on Divorce,"
    "Nighttime in the Country of New Mothers," "Home, I Say,"
    "This," "The Muse Gets Angry Before Leaving for School"
Paterson Literary Review: "Here is This Picture"
The Pedestal Magazine: "Washington Square, 1982," "Midsummer,"
    "1971, Winter in Queens," "Route 2"
Poetry East: "Taking It In"
Ploughshares: "Retelling"
Seneca Review: "Edvard Munch's Puberty, Mine," "Vestige"
Schuylkill Valley Journal of the Arts: "Her Window"
Tattoo Highway: "All in Black on the Streets of New York"
Tiferet: "When the Man You Love is a Blind Man"
Women Writers: "Meanwhile," "August, 1990," "Note to Self"
Wordgathering: "There Among the Haves," "Twelve Years Old,
    Swimming," "Stride Rite," "Nightbrace," "No," "At Fifteen
    Months," "Precedent"

"In a Campus Library" appeared in the *2010 Her Mark Calendar* juried by Maureen Seaton (Woman Made Gallery, 2010).

"No," "Because You Can't See My Photographs," and "Hemiplegia II" as "Hemiplegia" appeared in the anthology *Beauty is a Verb: The New Poetry of Disability,* edited by Jennifer Bartlett, Sheila Black, and Michael Northen (Cinco Puntos Press, 2011).

"When the Man You Love is a Blind Man" appeared in *Challenges for the Delusional,* edited by Christine Malvasi (Jane Street Press, 2012) and was republished in *Wordgathering.*

"In Rockaway," "Taking It In," and "Before Books" as "Why Books" appeared in the chapbook, *Left Standing,* (Finishing Line Press, 2005).

"Boy Child" and "The Impatient Mother" appeared in the anthology *Literary Mama: Reading for the Maternally Inclined,* edited by Andrea J. Buchanan and Amy Hudock (Seal Press, 2005).

"This" appeared in *Use Your Words: a Writing Guide for Mothers* by Kate Hopper, Viva Editions, 2012.

An earlier version of "Beach 27th Street" appeared in the anthology *You Are Here: New York City Streets in Poetry,* edited by Peggy Garrison, Victoria Hallerman and David Quintavalle (P&Q Press, 2006).

SPECIAL THANKS

Special thanks to Stephen Dunn, Douglas Goetsch, Aimée Harris, Julia Hough, Molly Peacock, Lynne Shapiro, and Daniel Simpson for their invaluable feedback on my poems; to Kay Vorhies for seeing what was missing; to Peter Murphy for his inspiring prompts; and to Michael Northen for his unflagging support of my work. Deep gratitude to Juan Alberto Pérez for allowing me to place his beautiful painting on the cover of this book.

For Ethan and Dan

CONTENTS

Three: Wings

ONE: HER WINDOW

IN ROCKAWAY

I have been out of the water
three years, breathing air.
They have placed me waist deep,
my bottom hanging in the familiar wet
like a conch shell.
Beside me, standing rooted and tall,
father, uncle.
I do not yet know they are brothers.
I do not yet know I am here
because one of them entered water,
pulled me out.
In front of us water lifts
like a greedy tongue that could take me back.
I yell, "Over my head, it's over my head"
and the men laugh,
raise me by the arms
into the air between them.
I think it's magic to be lifted whole-bodied,
magic that they do it each time, saving my life.
I do not yet know this is my element,
run, like I am, by the moon.
I do not yet know I will come here,
sucking the salt from my hair,
loving the slap of waves on my bones,
letting it drip with a tap down my back.
I do not yet know I will come here
in dark hours with other men,
finding the water
I began collecting inside me on this day,
making it rise, dance, begin to seep.

RETELLING

The sun was nothing more than an orange
the day Lisa ran for the ice cream truck.
It was small and even if it held sweetness,
even if it seeped Vitamin C, it couldn't stop
the car from barreling down Mott Avenue,
couldn't shine enough to show the driver
the seven year old girl dashing in front of his
Pontiac so that his foot would choose the brake.
The trees that saw it happen were no more
than rakes upended. They had no leaves
to form shadows. They had no song.
For a long moment, doorknobs
were merely ornamental. Those of us still
in our houses stayed in our houses.
I, five at the time, kept watching cartoons
while the sun watched over us and the trees
turned into notebooks so the story could change.

BEACH 27TH STREET

Summer evenings the aging couples
left supper dishes and snowy TVs to stroll
the sweet smelling slats of the boardwalk
where the ocean swelled like an inhaling belly
or rose to smash down froth depending
on its mood. Elsewhere,

(and elsewhere could be walked to)
were boarded buildings,
rumored drive-bys, white flight.
But here, on this street that touched
the water, small peninsula within the larger,
the doors were still unlocked.

HEMIPLEGIA I

I was maybe five when I first tried
to make sense of it, my split self,
the side that recognizes everything it touches,
the side that feels muted, slept on.
Why do I feel less on the right?
I wondered aloud and with the swiftness
of someone who's been waiting to be asked,
my mom said, *Your heart's on the left.*
Like everyone's. We were headed somewhere
in our blue Barracuda, my father focused
on the road, my mother gazing out
the passenger window as she defined the world.
I sat in back, the middle spot, feet on the hump,
left hand feeling for the ordinary drumbeat
I shared with every other living soul,
right not feeling much of anything at all.

NIGHT BRACE

With the ease of a salesman
she slips my shoe on nightly,
heel pressing her palm.
The brace, cool metal,
buckled at my ankle and knee.
The sales pitch, I could say with her:
Everybody's got something.
People wear glasses.
Ann Ratshin's daughter caught polio
swimming in a lake upstate.
In the dark I play with words.
Palsy, a tall pansy. *Polio,*
ring-o-leavio on pogo sticks.
When I move my foot, the quilt
rips a bit. When I feel it itch
I think I must be healing.

BEFORE BOOKS

"I've got the dirt on Ruth", my mother says
and I, crouched beneath the table,
picture her lifting the lid off her friend's
hamper to breathe the stale smell of the clothes.

But of course she's talking dirt
that travels cleanly through phone lines
from ladies like her who give away
everyone's secrets. Who, even as they offer
advice, rehearse the words they'll use,
select the people to tell.

Mean, I think, working
the stiff legs of Barbie into capris.
Still, I'm drawn into the thick
twists of a good story
as the hushed shuffle of slippers,
the stretched tail of the phone cord,
make their way from sink to stove.

1971, WINTER IN QUEENS

Pigeon-colored slush piles line the road.
Rain patters against the windshield.
I watch the drops eat one another
on their slow trip down the glass, notice
the closed car smells tart, like green apples.
My father's knuckles look burnt when we pass
the florescent signs of shops in strip malls,
his grip a tight fist on the wheel. At nine,
I know I won't find beauty on tired
Mott Avenue. No saints on the sagging
front porches, no slender whitewashed
birch trees to light the forest of such nights.

EDVARD MUNCH'S PUBERTY, MINE

I know the slump of those small shoulders
from the inside out. Eyes wide. Breast-buds
facing away from each other as if in shame.

Not that, at twelve, I posed naked for a painter.
Instead I wore a paper gown, gave myself
to the expert prodding of doctors.

One wished to move a muscle in my ankle
from front to back, elongate a heel too
stubborn to stretch on its own. *Whatever*

you think is best, my father said, if not
in words then nods. Only my mother braved
a question. *Will she still limp?* A pause.

Her limp will be different. Had anyone
asked me what I wanted, I wouldn't have
known to answer, *Keep me intact.*

I want my clothes back, I might have said.
Meanwhile, words poured over and around me
(*Extensor, Palsy, She, Her…*)
like I was a picture hanging on the wall.

ROCKING HORSE RANCH

My father, an expert rider, joined me
on the line for the beginner's trail
when he saw how scared I felt.
(It was the height, the large muscles
shifting beneath me, the way the horses
flicked their string mop tails at flies...)
Even so, I panicked, got down,
wound up waiting at the stalls.
Here is a picture of love:
a man, clomping behind dozens
of other people's kids
when he could have been flying, trees
a blur, breeze a thing of his own creation.
My dad who, at home, sat tethered
to the TV, should have come back
breathless that day, flushed,
barely recognizable.

TWELVE YEARS OLD, SWIMMING

Awkward in new angles and curves,
I could swim, slough all that off.
Sleek dolphin, mermaid grace

in the bright false blue of the pool
that changed from unbearably cold
to just warm enough once I dipped

my shoulders in. Light, afloat, I exhaled
bubbles, filled my head with humming
and watched my blurred familiar limbs

until shivering and famished, I rose
thinking, warm towel, salted fries,
ready to want the things of this world.

PASSING

She walks as if favoring a sore foot
and her one hand can't distinguish
coins from stones. Mostly, she imagines,
no one knows. At last week's dance, a boy
with sleek hair kissed her in the corner.
Tonight, her youth group is doing a yearly
good deed. Leaning on a wall, she watches
guests crowd the gymnasium in wheelchairs.
Skewed legs wrack with sudden currents.
Arms lay folded and stiff like cooked wings.
Her friends hold the twisted hands in their own
then sway, grace amid the wheels. She'll choose
a partner among the palsied strangers
when there's a song she can get lost in.
It will be like dancing with her secret self.

STRIDE RITE

I've managed to dream my way
back to that florescent lit house
of denial, house of oxfords
with good support. See me there,
five years old, near the Formica
counter, begging for Mary Janes.
And here, pouting in a corner chair
at twelve, over a pair of brown suede
clogs. My nemesis, that salesman
in the ill-fitting suit. Notice how
he straddles his slant-board seat
almost obscenely, my slender
teenaged toes pointing directly
to his crotch. He's merely a footman
but with power to declare *Not*
for you and *Maybe next year.* (Liar.)
Sorry, Princess, no sexy glass sling backs
for handicapped girls today.
I turn to my father who's here
to press his thumb above my big toe.
He watches, grim faced, as dozens of me
pace the colorless rug, my awful walk
and the shoes I so don't want
reflected in every mirror on the wall.

HERE IS THIS PICTURE

Oskar, stranger who left just as I was coming in.
They gave me the O from your name
which, like its thinner twin zero, is merely a hole
where, Grandfather, you could have been.
As it is, I've never known your generous lap,
the cigar store smell of your vest, never heard
your voice, its accent Yiddish or maybe New Yorkese.
Yet here is this picture and I love the man in it
holding my grandmother's hand.
You rest your chin on the shelf of her shoulder,
press your thumb into her palm.
Yours are the eyes of a man who is home now,
who long ago found within his plain wife
a beautiful girl who had hoped against hope to be seen.

BORDER SONG

Yaj cured me of my taste
for bad boys when we kissed
at our tenth grade beach party,
someone's staticy transistor
ruining an Elton John song,
the crackling bonfire
giving our clothes and hair
a sweet burnt smell.
Later, he bragged to his friends
that my nipples grew hard
when he grazed them
like it was his sloppy tongue
and not the ocean chill
that made them into little beads.
I wrote his real name, *Jay*,
in the sand with a stick
and erased it, then wandered
to the water's lacy edge.
Away from the others,
I wondered how it felt to kiss
a boy and *feel* something, how
it felt to kiss a boy who mattered.
High school's half over!
kids shouted, dancing
in the orange light of the fire.
I half wanted to go back
to that first untouched September.
I half wanted all of this
to hurry up and end.

TAKING IT IN

Somewhere, I am still seventeen,
sealed in my father's blue Barracuda,
hearing out his anger.
I am still being told
how I used to be good,
how they used to trust me,
now, I'm a stranger.
I'm still sticking
to the stitched white vinyl,
avoiding the eyes, their glint,
beer bottles on the sand.
Still, he's saying a man of twenty
only wants one thing
and when I get pregnant
don't come running to him.
I am still that girl who can't explain
why my insides rise like tide
when I park by the beach to kiss.
I'm still leaning my head
on that streaked glass
taking it in—
how unfair a man is,
this man, the first one I loved.

EIGHTEEN

We never spoke of what my body
couldn't do, so when Jen and Kay
left to pick apricots from the spindly tree
behind the library, I hesitated.
But Rich would be there.
I showed up in a wraparound skirt,
my excuse to stand at the base,
pluck from the bottom branch.
The fruit was concentrated at the top.
While the others climbed, of course
it was Rich I watched, squinting
up at him as I had all summer.
The night before, he'd finally
kissed me, his tongue tentatively
grazing my own. *Catch*, he called
now and I lifted my skirt to form
a net, no thought to palsy, to exposing
my uneven legs. When the first
tangy oval dropped into the voile
I had already begun to taste it,
how it felt to be chosen. And whole.

IN A CAMPUS LIBRARY

with thanks to Maxine Kumin
for Making the Jam Without You

There were blackberries on boil
in the book I held that afternoon,
a woman alone in a fragrant kitchen,
and beyond the house, horses
in tight stalls, though I knew this
from a different poem. In this one,
a girl my age slept in another time zone,
far from the rituals of sweetening,
boxes of pectin, mason jars washed
and waiting in rows. Rereading now,
I live in the skin of the mother,
the volume of silence in my child's
absence overwhelming the room.
But at nineteen, I was still a daughter,
fresh from Queens where the jam
we ate was store bought on sliced white.
Yet, crouched in those quiet stacks
I suddenly felt homesick as I tasted
the word *brambles* on my tongue.

HER WINDOW

So this is not a film. And she
is not star-like. Just a student,

flushed from having rushed
to catch the train. Through her

headphones, a soulful voice
and slow guitar. A soundtrack

to make even this uneventful
ride seem a pivotal scene.

The conductor lets his touch
linger when he takes her

crumpled money. A boy with
legs so long they live in the aisle,

turns to flash her a smile.
Darkened by evening, her window

reflects a girl whose hair falls
in waves, her throat delicately

framed by the line of her blouse.
What if this is it?

Her one moment when she is
at her ripest and most beautiful?

The conductor punctures another
person's ticket. The long legged

boy laughs into a tiny phone.
She fingers a button to replay her song.

WASHINGTON SQUARE, 1982

Walk through Washington arch and anything
might happen. First day breaking eighty.

You, a girl of twenty. High tops, no Mabelline,
sundress flowing like fountain water

down your thighs. Men swallow swords.
Magic Zack levitates his cigarette.

Boys on skateboards leap off ledges,
land like cats. You listen for his guitar, find him

singing *Sweet Melissa* to a slew of willing girls.
Today it's you who wins his crooked smile.

At *Heaven's Door* you add your voice
in perfect pitch. Potter's Field may lie beneath

your feet but you're pulsing, a wealth of summer
days before you, sun on your shoulders like mink.

MIDSUMMER

They're catching fireflies but the teens
in the grass are after each other.

Boys, jeans hanging from their hips,
break into sudden games of chase.

The girls, shoulders golden under
spaghetti straps, make a squealing show

of trying to escape. Mostly, they hover,
as easy to seize as the languid beetles

flicking their strobes. Captured, those
bugs have no more spark than houseflies.

Of course, foreshadowing gets lost in the dark
stand of trees and heat of midsummer

when you're sixteen and only just
discovering how you glow.

DOWNPOUR

Surely you've been there,
walking on a street at the start of your twenties
under a downpour so sudden you're drenched
moments after dismissing that first drop
as mere air conditioner spit on your skin.
Around you, people rush to cluster
beneath awnings and the narrow shelter of doorways.
But, though you can hear your mother's voice
urging you to follow,
it isn't cold, you haven't far, and in truth,
you like the weight of your sopping hair
and how your clothes cling
as though pressed by the flat of a hand.
So, while people have begun to stare, a man leers
and a child says, "she crazy", nudging his mother,
you keep your stride beneath the sky
of this particular day, taking what it has to offer.

ALL IN BLACK
ON THE STREETS OF NEW YORK

It camouflages fat. That and timidity.
Also subway grime, fear and the pastel optimism
you wore in high school. It's cover for the thick

books you've yet to read, the opaque philosophies
you only grasp in bits. It's an answer to the push pull
question, set yourself apart or blend. It belies

the open sky you miss, birdsong, your mom's roast
in thick brown gravy while you nibble virtuous
brown rice meals. It's for the guys, clad like you,

dark side out, who touch then leave your heart exposed.
It signifies insomnia, matches your coffee, says
this place that's braced for loss is now your home.

WE ARE EVERYWHERE

The first one I see, on Bleeker,
has a rigid leg that traces half moons
as she moves. The next, spotted on
Houston, uses crutches to swing
her whole self forward, a leap
for each of her boyfriend's strides.
Right now, a woman with auburn hair
and a gypsy skirt waits for the light
in a motorized chair. The walk sign
flashes green and, magnetized, I follow,
willing her to notice I'm kin.

TWO: GEODE

PRECEDENT

A boney dark haired girl
of twelve, I was new enough
at biking to feel wobbly
though I glided down
my own street, shade trees
watching like they always had.
Humming *Skyline Pigeon*
I flew, then flew into panic
at the speed I'd created
with my pumping feet.
The road narrowed
with parked cars and I
pressed my eyes shut.
Breath held, flowered
banana seat digging
into my tenderest place,
I careened. Yet nothing
happened. No crash, no fall.
No wonder I do it still,
let dumb luck drive.

THAT HAND

I wanted to show him the first house
I'd ever lived in, though it wasn't much,
a bungalow, really, wood broken off
in places, white paint dirtied to gray.
Still, it was part of my story like I hoped
he would be, so I paused there, rousing
a mangy dog who'd been sleeping
in the shadows, and who, if I remember right,
wasn't gated in or chained. As he lunged
in our direction I grabbed the hand
of that young man and held it,
even after the dog lost interest, melding
again with the shade. That hand
in that moment felt like it belonged
to a person who could save me if he had to,
who would choose to do so. This is how
it happens sometimes. You mistake someone
for an idea you have and settle for that.
It's like marrying a trick of the light.

AUGUST, 1990

I sit in the stilled car,
feet in tan sandals on the dash,
gauzy dress gathered to my knees.
It is two o'clock, the hour
we are supposed to be married.
But the justice is late and the young man
beside me taps a beat on the steering wheel,
studies an airplane's vapor trail
like a chalk line drawn across the sky.
Lifting a can of juice to my lips,
I think about the flowers wilting in the back seat
and how fully I want to love.
Of course, anything one does fully
is a journey alone. But I don't yet know this.
Not once do I glance at the dangling keys.

IN JERSEY NOW

From where I stand my old home
is a backdrop, the Chrysler
in its layers of tiaras, Empire
State, a candleholder for a single
candle, a single wish. Nights, the city
lights become my constellations,
a consolation for the endless stars
their bright life drowns out.
And what about this river?
What is it in the dark but an ink splat,
the story of my passage to this other,
tamer side, with all the lines I recognize
as fiction emphatically crossed out.

AFTER THE ULTRASOUND

It stood out like the lit
silhouette of a domed building
in what was otherwise
a Polaroid of mist. Assertive
as penises are at their best
and at their very worst.
The whole ride home
on the subway, I held
the tiny photo in my palm,
my other hand on the new
rounded place that housed
this forming boy. *A boy.*
Before I reached my stop,
he had a name. I said it
aloud, wondering what
countless other surprises he
had in store, what ratio of
love and heartbreak lay ahead.

BIRTH ROOM MIRROR

The head unfurls
into its solid shape.
I see his unfamiliar face,
its stillness like milk
calm in its cup.
An eye opens. A pause.
And he releases his voice,
startling himself with its force.

NO

The nurses shaped us into positions.
Cradle hold, football hold. My hands
couldn't take you to the right place.
Cerebral palsy I mumbled, apology,
explanation. As though those experts
of the body didn't already know.
Finally, they propped cushions around us.
Your lips touched my breast
but instead of suckling, you dozed.
This had the nurses worried.
I worried how I'd feed you alone.
That night, your wail woke me.
I scooped you up, found the nurse's bell.
When a new one came, I shyly
explained the pillows, the palsy.
"No," she said coolly and I stared.
"No. That baby needs sleep not milk"
I tried again: "he's hungry."
Shaking her head, she left our room.
I attempted the football hold.
The cradle. Tried setting up pillows
then sitting between them. They fell.
Keeping you in my arms, I paced, I sang.
We cried in unison, both of us
so helpless, so desperately new.

NIGHTTIME IN THE COUNTRY
OF NEW MOTHERS

Night spills its ink
and few citizens notice,
here where sleep is just memory and hope,

moments stolen upright in a rocker;
the woozy feel of not enough, a way of life.
Here, women pace, speak in whispers

and in high unfamiliar voices that are almost song.
Held so they'll rest, the babies feel warm, wilted.
Their smell sour but sweet

the way fear and love are indistinguishable
as together they govern the lamplit rooms.
Hour upon hour, the mothers study

these new ancient faces:
lashes and brows, wet demanding mouths,
the visible pulsing of veins.

Harm, we think, conjuring falls, bruises,
the near silent rhythm of breath stilled.
Cries rising from windows are mostly the babies,

but, rocking and nursing, some mothers weep too.
We were merely girls before crossing this border,
our empty arms impossibly light.

HOME, I SAY

From the wash, I pull a shirt
the size of a dinner napkin,
stretch the opening at the neck
so as not to frighten him
with too long a moment blinded by cloth.
So many mistakes I can make, and I do.
The worst, catching a bit of his skin
between the locked halves of a snap.
Cries can be stoppered most times
by the sudden milk my body makes,
suck and swallow the only sound
beside the rhythmic thump of our chair.
Blue eyes drinking me in, I feel
compelled to name things for him.
Window and *bear. Sunlight* and *reading lamp.*
Home, I say, as though this place
is not a splintered boat.
And, *Daddy,* as though this person
is not already taking leave.

FEVER SPIKE

For Dr. J. Pérez

My child is ablaze and, because it's not the first time,
I'm efficient. A dropper-full of sticky Motrin

smelling like candy on his lips. Tepid water
in the tub. I climb in with him like we're one being,

the hot slack infant and I. His mouth finds my breast
while I douse his hair with bath water. *Keep the head cool*

I hear in our doctor's soothing baritone. I'd rather think
of that voice than the baby's burning head. The fontanel

still closing, brain abuzz, and all that trust. In truth,
I'm telling my first lie to him, calmly singing Brahm's

Lullaby in the heat of this moment as though no harm
could ever come while he's in the cradle of my arms.

MEANWHILE

I want to know I can keep something alive
my husband said, having brought home
a cactus. Small, thumb-shaped, it lived
by his computer. If he ever watered it,
I couldn't say. He was out most nights by then.
And me, I was up so often nursing.
One day, his plant sprouted a flower,
a bright red dot like a blood spot
on that digit. Happy, he danced
through our kitchen in a way
I once found charming. Meanwhile,
the baby had grown a milk-tooth,
learned to raise his arms for me
to lift him, responded
with wet smiles when I sang his name.

AT FIFTEEN MONTHS

My son works his way
from the far end of the kitchen.
New to walking, his halting
steps, mostly on tip-toe,
resemble my own palsied gait.
Soon, I know, he'll steady
himself, easily outrace me.
But just now, his face, flushed
with effort, seems backlit.
Mama, he chimes, tilting
precariously toward me.
Crouched against the wall,
I brace myself for his weight
and, I admit, savor it, this flicker
of time when he's a little less
perfect, a little more mine.

FAMILY BED

He's found his way into our bed again,
one small elbow dangerously close to my eye.
And though I barely fit the sliver of middle
you two back sleepers leave me,
I let him stay, turning sometimes
toward his jutting unpredictable angles,
sometimes toward the pungent skin
beneath your raised arm. Crushed between
your sleep and his, what I feel for the moment
is sated. For here in the brightening dark,
everything I breathe and that's pressed
against my flesh weights me
to the fragrant tangle that we've made.

FROM THE LIST OF REASONS

This was at his father's funeral.
He spoke at the podium
and from the pews, sniffling,

shaky laughter, a low cry
from my own throat when he noted
the children he'd one day have

would never know their granddad.
My kids, I thought and tasted tears.
Afterwards, he looked for me.

Over a slow sea of heads
I saw him craning, calling.
My name a question

he repeated and repeated
until I broke through, reaching up
to hold his wide trembling back.

For a decade, I lay with that back pressed
against me in the dark, often recalling
how lost he seemed on that hardest of days.

It's one reason I stayed.

MR. ROGERS

Such comfort, that same
zippered sweater, slippers
he'll toss once in the air
before untying his Keds.
From the cupboard, glitter
and crayons in a shoe box.
A project that will look like
what it is, folded paper
and pieces of tape. Restless,
my child slaps his alphabet
blocks on the table,
tears me from that calm,
that paneled room, the one man
who was ready to forgive
before I'd even made my mistakes.

VESTIGE

My husband has a new theory.
He tells me I don't have to have
cerebral palsy, that it's my choice.
What do you say to something like that?
I watch him chug juice directly
from the carton, his flawless body
blocking the light of our open fridge.
The boy I married claimed
he loved my weaker hand,
because—his words—it could never
hurt anyone. He said that. He did.
I still have the kiss on my palm.

THE NIGHT WE DECIDE ON DIVORCE

Our son sleeps beneath his quilt
with the bright triangle fish,
his stuffed dog tossed and trapped
between the mattress and wall.
Water warms to the temperature of air
in its plastic cup by the bed
and clothes still smelling of juice and sun
lay heaped on their corner of floor.
His shelves of toys
form their usual shapes in the dark
while he breathes in a rhythm
mealtime, playtime, bath
like the day he rests from
and the day he expects
come morning.

ROUTE 2

Why is divorce so expensive,
Lynn asks, fiddling with the radio dial.
Because it's worth it, we both say,
laughing louder than we should
with our boys asleep, cheeks pressed
against the vinyl of their car seats.
Soon, I'll have to give mine his dinner,
a bath, read five picture books.
But for now, I watch Lynn throw
her head back to sing with Aretha,
note that yes, forty still looks good
and the traffic moves perfectly to this song.
Billboards flip past like flashcards
then we hit a stretch of unbroken green
as the wind through our open windows
sends my hair every which way
making a gorgeous mess of it.

BOY CHILD

The stray ballpoint, a gun.
Umbrella, a sword.
Hands empty,
the air gets a roundhouse kick.

Is this typical '*boy*' I want to ask.
Or just typical of *this* boy?
Past bedtime he's enacting battles,
strategies elaborate as chess rules.

Finally, he crash-lands beside me,
seeks my shoulder, slurs "Mommy..."
I stroke his sweat-damp hair
until, shifting position, he sleeps,
arms thrown back in surrender.

THIS

Already, he has fallen head first
off the back of the couch,
held a rusted nail in his mouth
without swallowing it down.
I keep the television black,
newspapers folded on the porch.
Still, the stories find me. Airplanes
fall from the sky with children in them.
A young man hikes into the mountains
and is never found. One night, my son
takes the hand of another four year old
and runs across a thoroughfare.
If I'd left him what he was, a thought,
I wouldn't have become this,
a crazy woman whispering thank you
to unseen beings in the air.

GEODE

My four-year-old picks this,
the homeliest of stones,
out of all the treasures
in the museum gift shop.
Though it looks like an egg
made from a slab of sidewalk,
he grasps it in his dimpled hand.
At home, I put it in an old sock
and let him pound it with a mallet.
All of this thrills him,
the noise, the destruction,
and finally the discovery.
Beauty can be jagged.
A broken thing can shine.

WEEKEND FAIR

The Ferris wheel is small, rickety,
shorter than the squat houses beside it.
So when it stops with my child at the top,
no one panics. Without strain, I call to him,
see the thrill of slight fear glowing on his face.
A man speaks to a crackling radio in his palm
and with a squeak of slicker and boots,
a fireman appears for what must be the best
kind of rescue. A step ladder and he's a hero,
lifting the child in his strong arms, placing him
down by my side. I take the boy's sticky hand,
walk him through a din of arcade bells, vendors,
groups of teens with green fluorescent circles
on their chests. We move toward the dark,
listening night while he tells and retells the story.
The Ferris wheel gaining height. His time in the sky
stretching out until it seems he waits there still,
his old life growing vague and insignificant below.

KERIAH

My rabbi offers to pin a loop of ribbon
to my bodice. Its function, to be torn
in place of the cloth. But this time,
I want to rip the thing itself, my thrift shop
Donna Karan with its squared neckline,
its seams that hug my hips. I watch as he
leans into the space between us, the place
reserved for such intimate acts. His face
knots with effort as he splits the corner
near my right shoulder. *There,* he says
and we nod under a sky just beginning
to bruise. I finger the small break
in the fabric, one another woman might
stitch, cover with a broach. I plan
to toss the black heap in the trash
since I've run out of parents to bury
and I won't ever dance in this dress.

TESTING THE SEAMS

I think of the Hulk, that bulging creature
outlined on my son's green t-shirt.
It barely fits him anymore,
now that his father's body asserts itself in him,
widening the plain between his shoulder blades,
fleshing out his thighs. What *pulkas*,
my mother would say were she here to pinch them.
His legs are suddenly log solid.
Their stance, a man to be reckoned with.
Understand, there was a man I learned
I couldn't live with, who couldn't live with me.
Yet here he is, testing the seams of my son's clothing,
refusing to keep to the confines of my past.

SLOW COOKER STEW

I rinse, peel, slice potatoes,
cut into an onion, wiping my burning eyes
with the back of my hand. I once believed
onions channeled sad thoughts,
whispering like oracles, *your mother*
will die one day, your father, you.
Easy to imagine wizardry from root vegetables
back when the kitchen was my parents' domain.
Not that magic doesn't happen now.
Tomorrow, already late for work,
I'll pile these pieces into a ceramic crock,
add stew meat, a can of soup, then simply
flip a switch. Six o'clock, the aroma
of a simmering meal will meet me at the door
and I can feel, in that one moment at the threshold,
like somebody's daughter again, or somebody's wife.

DOWAGER'S HUMP

Once again, I am
thinking of your body,
the master copy for my own.
When was it
that your back first bent
to form a question mark?
And, Mom, what question
held you so much in its clasp
in those last years
that you asked it
with your whole self?

THE IMPATIENT MOTHER

I know it in my teeth when I become her,
the way they tingle, tighten against each other,
and in my sudden rod straight spine.
Beside her at the table, my son twists away
from a sheet of questions on Lincoln.
He scuffs the floor with a squeak of sneakers,
whines, *this is hard.* She feels the pitch of his voice
on her scalp and, though I have poured tea,
wrapped her fingers around the heat of the cup,
she will not be calmed. *You're not trying,*
she accuses, barks *think!*, then marches to the sink
to wash dishes, clattering them onto the rack
to show what accomplishment sounds like.
Behind her she can hear sighs and the tick
of a pencil hitting wood. Such an actor, she thinks.
But when she turns to him again his shoulders
are shaking, his face wet. This is what it takes
for her to leave us alone. I dry my hands,
hold him, rub slow circles on his back.
He is still such a small boy. *Shhh,*
I whisper, as if I could erase her work.
You can do this. You can.

PORTRAIT

My ex never meant to take this picture.
Enjoying the heft of his new Nikon
he'd straddled the sill, shooting a passing parade.
Cub scouts, marching bands, pristine cars from the fifties.
"I want to slip in there a minute," I said. "Show the baby."

"Him, him, him," he flared and I felt it, as usual,
in my stomach. "It's always about him,"
Still, he relented, lent us the window,
photographed us taking our turn.

Proud of the results, he blew it up, framed it,
yet never questioned my choice
to claim it when we divided our things.

The portrait could have been commissioned,
it's so beautiful. Soft blur of black and white,
the inviting emptiness of silhouettes.
And the negative space, shaped by the tilt
of a mother's gaze toward her infant,
that takes the form of wings.

THREE: WINGS

THERE AMONG THE HAVES

A girl with one prosthetic leg dances
at a club in short skirt and heels
on the cover of *SundayStyles*, her
silver thigh textured like sequins,
hair over her face, not to hide
but she's lost in that song.
I tape her photo next to my desk,
recall the morning I had my new love
touch my calves, the right thin
with palsy, the other, full and strong.
That same day we kissed like teens
in a New York café, his guide dog
curled like a throw rug at our feet.
"Anyone else making out?" he asked.
"Just us," I said, eyeing an indifferent
crowd. And there, among the haves,
those with sight, with matching limbs,
he whispered that my breasts spell
a perfect C in braille. So this is how
it feels, I thought, to inherit the earth,
how it feels loving one of my own.

BECAUSE YOU CAN'T SEE
MY PHOTOGRAPHS

I seek out the past in voices, pulling you over
to speak with men whose words are edged
with my father's New Yorkese, or to hear songs
I listened to in the family car. Sometimes,
I name shapes to convey what I mean. *Bowl*
for the feeling of standing surrounded by
mountains as a teen, *torpedo* for the rounded
point my pregnant belly made a decade before
we met. Once, I placed a friend's infant on your lap,
telling you my son had been heavier than she,
that his scalp smelled like sleep lingering in sheets.
I have box after box of pictures, curled rectangles
that are blank to you. Still if you could travel
back to the schoolyard in Queens where I played
as a child, I trust you'd recognize the girl I was,
you who tease her laugh from me so easily.

TO TEARS

A country song praising broken roads,
Virginia Woolf's prose. My list is long.
Anger reduces me. Old hurts. Surprise.
My come-cry sometimes comes with sobs.
Crying solves nothing, my mother would say.
Her admonishment, *be strong*. Ignore that voice.
Today, my son crumbles against my shoulder,
having been called to the office at school,
wrongly accused. I let it rack through his body,
rub that back. Emptied, he'll sleep deeply tonight,
as he will someday after making love, as he did
in his first weeks when crying was the only means
he had to speak or call love into a room.

WHEN THE MAN YOU LOVE
IS A BLIND MAN

You can stop shaving your legs
when the temperature drops
and he'll say he likes a change
in texture with the seasons. You can
leave that bit of silver in your bangs.
Your fashion advice will be gospel.
When he tells you you're beautiful,
you'll know he's talking about
something in you that's timeless,
something about you that's true.
If, teasing, he says that smearing color
on your face is what a clown does,
explain how a touch of blush
can change the feel of entering a room
and he'll listen. He'll always listen
like the wide world is a raft with only
two people on it and he finds you
the more interesting of the two.
Imagine going with him to the Rockies.
He hears you sigh and asks
what the mountains look like. All you have
are words. *Awesome. Grandeur.*
But when you describe that feeling
of seeing your one life for the flicker it is,
he knows. *Oh*, he says. *Oh.*
It's like hearing music in a cathedral.

FIRST ANNIVERSARY

Once, as a child, I had my father
close his eyes for a surprise
then, distractedly, walked him
into a wall. Now, guiding you,
I know to mention each curb, each
puddle to be stepped over, to place
your palm on the chipped rail
beside the subway stairs before
I follow you down. All the while,
the tip of your folded white cane
peeks from the side pocket of your pack
like something inner and exposed.
We've spent this year learning one
another. One night, you asked the color
of my hair then repeated the word brown,
an abstract fact to be memorized.
The dark strands were splayed
on your chest as I listened
to the beat beneath skin and rib
and thought about trust, your life
in your hand given over to mine.

JUST THIS ONCE

I want to rest my head on your chest
and listen to the rhythmic pump
of blood without thinking how distant
it sounds, how meek. How a music box
always winds to a stop mid-song.

QUESTION AND ANSWER

Why am I an only child, my son asks
and all day the question beats inside me
the way everything that has ever troubled
him does. The dead gerbil, canceled sleepover,
my own brusqueness and impatience most of all.
A cacophony made of the shadows that cross
my one boy's open face. Why is the heart alone
in the chest? I want to offer in response.
Where would I fit another such wrenching love?

AT NEWARK AIRPORT

This is its own kind of tragedy,
how casually my son slips off his sneakers
—a full three and a half sizes larger
than last year's—and places them in a bin
that, at home, might be filled with water
and used to wash the plates from our lunch.
Here, he understands, it's used to ensure
that he has no hidden wires in either of his soles,
no hidden plans to blow himself up,
and with him the rest of us shuffling along
this snake of a line in our stocking feet.
Such a thing is possible, he knows. It's been
attempted, perhaps somewhere by children
younger than he. Here, now, he's learned
everyone is suspect. The businessman
who dropped his coins while emptying his pockets,
the small gray-haired woman in pink sweats.
Even me, the one he still sometimes calls *Mommy*
in private, the one who brought him to this place.

MY TWELVE-YEAR-OLD RETURNS FROM CAMP HAVING LEARNED RIFLERY

He's always liked having something to hold,
a spoon raised like a scepter while I pushed
his stroller. Later, those Matchbox cars
and plastic action figures he dubbed *pocket toys*
though they lived in his sweaty palms.
Today he shows me a paper target, each
black rimmed hole smaller than a fingertip.
Most are close to center which means, of course,
he's good at this. When he was a newborn,
I watched his wild hands and thought of dandelions
bouncing on their stems. Even then,
while learning how to hold him, I'd begun
to understand a mother's other job, this letting go.

THE MUSE GETS ANGRY
BEFORE LEAVING FOR SCHOOL

I'm ruining my son's life by making him wear a jacket.
"I'll be hot all day," he yells, tugging the collar,
"It's too tight anyway." Slamming the door.

He's outgrowing everything. Jackets, pants,
my directives on what to wear. Another mother
would take this afternoon, shop for clothes

two sizes up. But in this silence I hear the start
of something, an image of stillness in the aftermath
of my growing boy's huff. Back in the birth room,

through a mirror, I saw his face seconds before
his body. His expression: *Calm as milk in its cup.*
In its own cup, my tea grows cold.

HEMIPLEGIA II

Left, my bright half, gets all of it...
soft sharp prickly wet lined.
But press your head against my right shoulder,
I sense weight but no warmth. Your cheek,
to my right touch, stubble free,
whether or not you shave.
Under my right fingers your silver hair
holds no silk, nor can I feel it part
into single strands. I'll tell you
how I know you in the dark.
Left whispers the details.
Right listens and believes.

NOTE TO SELF

Remember the peasant dress
with the pattern of small blue flowers
you loved when you were nine,
its ankle length skirt, puffed bodice,
elastic in the capped sleeves
that hugged your upper arms.
Sometimes Dan wraps his long
fingers at that same place
just below your shoulder.
Sometimes he whispers
into your middle-aged ear
words meant directly for that girl.
What can you know of the future?
There'll be shifts and losses
you'll contend with when you have to.
Put on something that makes you feel pretty.
Hold that man while he's yours.

SIX ROLLER COASTERS

Ethan pulls Dan, almost at a run,
toward those massive structures that rise
and dip like the outlines of distant hills.
Their plan, to conquer all of them
despite pounding rain. I read Hemingway
in the shelter of the food court
where they appear occasionally,
flushed and dripping in their ponchos,
to describe the fastest, the longest drop,
the one that whips like the tail
of the guide dog we left at home.
Thumb keeping place in my book,
I think about what men build
through shared bravery and fear,
and marvel at my twelve year old,
willing to hold Dan's hand in public
for this greater good. There are moments
on the *Storm Runner*, the *Fahrenheit*
when I know he closes his eyes
to see how it feels to Dan, this man
who might have been his father
had I a better time of it
early in my own wild ride.